DROPSHIPPING A BEGINNER'S GUIDE TO DROPSHIPPING

HOW TO MAKE MONEY ONLINE AND BUILD YOUR OWN ONLINE BUSINESS

JAMES MOORE

CONTENTS

MY GIFT FOR YOU

My Top Dropshipping Suppliers

Click for Free Access

I've compiled over 30 of my personal dropshipping suppliers that I've used before, based on their quality and ability. Taking the guess work out of who to choose!

INTRODUCTION

Welcome to the world of drop-shipping. I want to extend a very warm welcome to you for joining me here today. I'm James Moore, and I am going to help to shed some light on this huge and vast, wealth-creating topic.

I believe Drop-shipping is the perfect business to get your feet wet when it comes to making money online. Then once you have built your confidence you can either continue and expand or like myself venture into multiple business ventures.

Opening an online business couldn't be easier than it is today. With the development of Amazon, eBay, Shopify, and the many other online retail platforms, anybody who has around $50 can start an online store, realistically speaking. And this is fantastic news.

If you're just beginning, you might not have significant cash reserves or a large area or warehouse for the storage of your goods. As an aside, it can be intimidating to figure out what the best thing is to sell. This is where drop-shipping and drop-shipping supplier directories is such an attractive avenue for making money.

In this title, we'll take the guess work out of drop-shipping. It's so much easier when you know what you're up against. So, again, I thank you for joining me here, and I hope you find all of the informational super-helpful to you. If you can take some time to learn and build up your knowledge on this topic, then you're halfway there already! Let's get started...

1

WHAT IS DROPSHIPPING?

DROPSHIPPING IS A METHOD OF RETAIL FULFILLMENT WHERE AN online store doesn't hold its sellable products in stock. In fact, when a store sells an item, it will purchase this item directly from a third party where they have it shipped directly to the customer. Therefore, this method takes out the legwork involved in needing storage for products, the need for packing, and the time and products necessary for posting.

The most noteworthy difference between dropshipping and a standard retail model is that the selling merchant doesn't stock or own any inventory (a list of stocked goods). As an alternative, the merchant (you) would purchase inventory as is needed from a third party which is usually a wholesaler or manufacturer to fulfill their customers' orders. This can be done via a website, a self-created store (like Shopify) or a platform geared up for merchants, like eBay or Amazon.

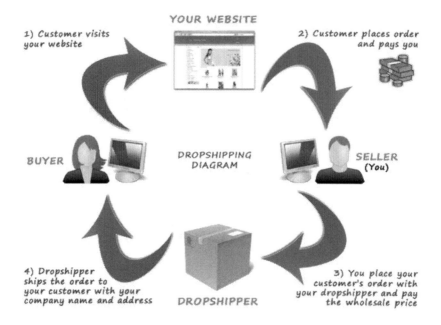

Manufacturers, Wholesalers, and Dropshippers: What's the Difference?

A manufacturer is: the real producer of a product. As an example, Nintendo manufactures the Wii console.

A wholesaler: buys directly from a manufacturer and resells the products to retailers, adding on their gain to make money.

A dropshipper is: anyone who will ship an item directly to your customer on your behalf.

It is possible that both manufacturers and wholesalers might become dropshippers, too. If you can find a manufacturer who will ship their product directly to your customers (rare) then they will, in fact, be acting as a dropshipper.

Likewise, a wholesaler who will send products directly to your customers on your behalf is also a dropshipper.

Choosing suppliers for your dropshipping enterprise can be one of the most crucial decisions you'll ever make. If your supplier makes mistakes, it's up to your accountability to make sure your customer is taken care of, not theirs. You need to make sure your choice of supplier is someone who can (and will) have your back while working to make your partnership grow. Overall the dropshipping model has some benefits and some drawbacks. Let's take a look at these now.

DROPSHIPPING BENEFITS

LESS CAPITAL IS REQUIRED

PERHAPS THE MOST ESSENTIAL ADVANTAGE TO DROPSHIPPING IS that it's possible to launch an e-commerce store without the need to invest thousands of dollars in inventory to start with. Customarily, merchants have had to tie up vast amounts of capital when acquiring stock. But, this is unnecessary if you use dropshipping.

With a dropshipping model, there is no need to purchase a product without you already having made the sale, and having been paid by your customer. Devoid of substantial up-front inventory investments, it is very possible to begin a thriving dropshipping business without minimal financial backup.

It's Easy to Start

Running e-commerce businesses is easier when you don't have to deal with handling physical products. When you dropship, you have no worries about:

- Paying for, or managing a warehouse

- Packing and shipping your customers' orders
- Tracking the inventory for accounting purposes
- Handling inbound shipments or any returns, physically
- Repeatedly ordering products and maintaining stock levels
- Needing a storage place to hold physical products

Low Overheads

Because there is no reason to deal with purchasing any inventory or the management of a warehouse, your overheads and businesses expenses can be quite small. Many successful dropshipping companies are run from home offices with a single computer for less than $100 per month. As your business grows, it's likely these expenses will increase, but nonetheless, they will still be low when compared to traditional brick-and-mortar companies.

Flexible Location Possibilities

Dropshipping businesses can be run from almost anywhere as long as you have an internet connection. This is vital to allow communication with your suppliers and your customers, both quickly and efficiently. Many successful online stores are run by people when they live outside of their home country, too.

A Vast Selection of Products

Because there is no need to pre-purchase any items you sell, you can offer a broader array of products to potential customers. So, if your supplier stocks a certain product, you can list it for sale in your online store, or on the platform you use, at no additional cost.

Ease of Scalability

With conventional business types, if you have orders for three times as much business, it is likely you'll need to perform three times as much work. With the leveraging of dropshipping suppliers, the majority of the work in processing additional orders is borne by your suppliers. This allows you to expand your business with fewer growing pains. Sales growth always brings some extra work. In most cases, this is primarily related to customer service. Companies that exploit dropshipping as a necessity, scale exceptionally well, especially when compared to conventional e-commerce businesses.

All of these benefits make dropshipping an advantageous and efficient model to both new and established merchants, alike. Regrettably, dropshipping isn't always a bed of roses, though. All this convenience and flexibility comes with a few disadvantages. Let's shed some light on these.

3

DISADVANTAGES

LOW MARGINS

Low margins are one of the most noteworthy downsides to operating in a competitive dropshipping niche. Since it's so easy to start, and overhead costs are minimal, many merchants set up their store and sell items at the lowest possible prices to grow revenue. But, because they invested so little in starting their business, they can only afford to function on minimal profit margins.

In many cases, these merchants have low-quality websites or storefronts. Customer service is poor, if any. Nonetheless, this doesn't stop customers comparing their prices to yours. The increase in ruthless competition will quickly obliterate any profit margins inside any given niche. Fortunately, you can do a lot to alleviate this problem by choosing a niche that's better suited for dropshipping. And, it's also important to always maintain your reputation with great customer service. This way, your customers will become loyal and gain trust in your business enterprise.

Balancing Inventory Issues

If you are in a position to stock your own items, it's comparatively straightforward to track things which are in and out of stock. However, when you source from numerous warehouses (which are probably also fulfilling orders for other merchants), their inventory can change on a daily basis. While there are methods of how to better sync your store's stock with your suppliers, these answers don't always work as seamlessly as expected, and your suppliers might not support the technologies which are required.

Shipping Complexity

If working with multiple suppliers as many dropshippers do, the products in your store will be sourced from various dropshippers. This might complicate shipping costs.

A good example is if a customer places an order for three items. These are available from separate suppliers, in this example. When they order, you will incur separate shipping charges from each of your suppliers. At this point, it isn't wise to pass these charges to your customer. They will quickly think you're overcharging for shipping. Average the costs out so you can maintain it, without losing money, or passing on these high costs to your customers.

Mistakes from Suppliers

Errors from your supplier will hurt your business. Suppliers might be cheap, yet if they use inferior packaging or continually pack the wrong orders, it is you who has to stand up and apologize. Additionally, the frustration which comes with incorrect shipments or damage is not fun to deal with if it happens all the time. This is true for you as a merchant, and for your customers, too.

WHERE TO LOOK FOR DROP SHIPPING SUPPLIERS

THERE ARE A NUMBER OF WAYS TO FIND DROP SHIP SUPPLIERS, but 3-4 main ways. In this section I'll cover the most common approaches to finding a supplier.

There are various ways to find dropshippers for your new business. I will cover some of them now:

1. Directly Contact the Manufacturer

If you know the product/s or brand/s you want to begin selling, a really great approach is to get in direct contact with the manufacturer who deals with them, directly. In fact, by doing this, you can easily get the cheapest possible pricing and also avoid the "middle man."

In some cases, the manufacturer might not have a dropshipping service in place, but in any case, they should be able to point you in the right direction, or even have some awesome contacts under their belt to get you started.

2. Google Searches

Another fantastic way of finding a great dropshipping supplier is by searching Google. This way you can hunt the online market, and if you're willing to work hard to find them, it can be a great method to use.

Sometimes, searching Google for suppliers can be difficult, because it's not always easy to find them. On many occasions, wholesale suppliers might have out of date websites that don't stay aligned with modern, search engine optimization tools. So, keep hunting, you may not find your perfect supplier on page 1. But, when you want the best one for your niche area, or if you need a particular brand of product, you won't mind searching just that little bit longer. While searching, you'll need to use a variety of terms like: "dropshipper," "wholesaler," "wholesale dropship," "supplier," "wholesale reseller," and/or "wholesale supplier."

3. Buy a Supplier Directory

While there are many dropshipping directories available online, most of them are of mediocre or low-quality, so they provide minimal value. But, there are some legitimate directories. I believe that the best sources can be found from online supplier directories. These can ascertain profiles from (literally) hundreds or thousands of manufacturers, wholesalers, and suppliers, alike.

4. Referrals

When you do start to uncover suppliers, even if they don't seem the perfect fit for you, you can still ask them if they can steer you in the right direction. Because they're already in the industry, this means they will probably have great contacts, and most won't mind referring you to someone that might be right for your express needs.

In addition, sometimes the best leads can come from referrals you get from your friends and family. Social networking and social media platforms have made everything really easy to get the word out through the use of these channels. So, look out for these too!

REACHING OUT TO A DROPSHIPPING SUPPLIER

THERE ARE SOME HELPFUL WAYS TO BEGIN REACHING OUT TO dropship suppliers. You can do this once you've created a small list of possible dropshipping wholesalers or manufacturers. Now is the time for you to reach out and see if they'll be a good fit for your online store.

Send a Courtesy Email First

A quick email can be the easiest way to make the first contact. Obtaining the information you require is easier via email than phone, and sometimes, you might be speaking to non-English speaking individuals.

Make sure a potential supplier comes across as being professional, and you obtain all the information you require. Supplier contact emails will save hours of your time and boost the likelihood that any supplier will actually respond to you. This is a great test of their communication ability.

Follow Up with a Phone Call

After you have sent an initial email to increase your chances of a good response, use a follow-up phone call. This can be a good way of checking how well their customer service personnel perform.

Prepare your List of Questions

The key to sounding like a professional and steeling your nerves is preparation, and being fully ready beforehand. When you ask questions, you quickly learn more about your supplier. It will show that you have done your homework if they appear to be a good fit.

Here are 10 Common Questions You Can Ask:

What are your payment terms, and are they negotiable?

This is fundamental. It will aid you in seeing their actual pricing strategy because prices listed on their website are (more often) higher than their regular rate, and what they actually charge merchants. Now you can haggle for the best deal.

Are there additional costs besides the purchase price?

There are many suppliers who charge delivery fees, fuel surcharges, fees for returns (restocking), or duties (import taxes) on imported goods. It is wise to know all these ahead of time. You need to factor in everything before you charge your customers.

Does your supplier sell direct?

On more than a few occasions, suppliers will sell directly to consumers as well as selling to dropshipping services. You should at least know this before you choose them, because if they do, this would mean you are in direct competition with your supplier. This could make things difficult and uncomfortable.

What are your return policies?

On a few occasions, your customers will make mistakes, and order the incorrect item. On other occasions, suppliers do accidentally ship the wrong item. It will happen, and it is one thing you need to know in advance. And how will your supplier handle these situations?

Does your supplier know your expected gross margin?

The gross margin is the amount of money you can make after you have sold something, minus the product cost to you. Even though you set your own price, your supplier should be able to advise what other resellers make, on average.

Are your prices likely to change?

It's pretty common for some suppliers to change prices on you without giving any advance notice. Any shift which is substantial and similar to this can be harmful to your business. It is for this reason that it's good to know if and when this might happen.

How good is the product's warranty or guarantee?

To offer customers a great return policy for faulty products, you need to know what kind of warranties your supplier gives you.

Can your service reps answer my questions about the product?

While this isn't 100% necessary, it's good to know how much you can rely on your supplier's sales staff to answer questions about the product. The more complicated the product is, the more important this is, too. Especially if it has technology involved with it.

Do you use data feeds?

It's good to know if your supplier does support data feeds so you can quickly update your store without the manual entering like quantity, descriptions, and images. This is much easier once you know how to utilize it.

Will your manufacturer let you customize their items?

Being a merchant who's there for the long haul, it's great to be creative. If you ever plan on creating your own unique products, you'll need a supplier or manufacturer who will customize your items.

How to Avoid Scams

Not all dropshippers have your ultimate interests in mind. Unfortunately, there is no scarcity of people out there looking to steal your money. However, there are a few ways to protect yourself, and ensure you never fall victim and get scammed. Let's take a look at them now.

Checking the Warning Signs

There are some red flags to watch out for when searching for a whole-sale dropshipping supplier:

Memberships or Monthly Fees

Some legitimate suppliers will charge monthly fees, but some are only looking to take your money. The most straightforward ways to avoid this fraud is to find out why these fees are charged. Honest? It probably is. The bottom line? Always do your research.

Refusing Checks or Credit

If your supplier only wants to deal strictly with bank transfers, it's time to turn in the opposite direction. 99% of serious suppliers will accept credit, or checks. SaleHoo automatically checks and displays all results regarding these metrics for you.

Hiding Their Address

All legitimate suppliers must display their business address. Anyone who doesn't show an address gives out a giant red flag. SaleHoo shows and lists all suppliers' addresses right on their profile page.

Not Being Listed (the US only) on the BBB

The Better Business Bureau is a US-based, non-profit organization which keeps businesses in check. With the BBB, people can go to report frauds, and the BBB will also take legal action against illegal or unethical companies. This can be a great way of seeing a business' dirty laundry if they have any.

This is an excellent source to check. The SaleHoo directory will automatically monitor and display all US suppliers' BBB ratings.

Action Steps to Avoid Fraud

Here are some further actions you can take to check each supplier on your potential supplier list:

Checking Their Domain Age

Young domain names more-than-likely mean a business is new, which might often indicate a scam. Most suppliers have been around for a good many years. The in-depth SaleHoo directory automatically displays the number of years a supplier has been in business. You can also check the domain age of supplier websites using the *Domain Age Checker* tool.

Use Google and Search for Them

If someone has a bad experience with a supplier, they more than likely highlight the fact and write about it online. The simplest way to locate these listings is by searching for the following: "[Supplier Name] + Scam" on Google, or other search engines. More often than not, if the supplier is running a scam, you'll be highlighted to the fact right away in the results.

Calling Them

One of the most unassuming and quickest ways to spot deceitful suppliers is by giving them a call. If you ask them some of the questions laid out in the earlier section, it can help your cause. You might find they stutter or find it difficult to begin answering your questions, and, if this is the case, it should raise red flags. In many instances, you might notice that the phone number doesn't even work.

Mapping Their Address

If a supplier address doesn't show up, or it isn't really their place of business, this can also be a cause for concern. Google maps can be great for checking out the street view to get a look at their building. Does the place appear in a distribution center or just a regular house? It might even be some other business type entirely. The SaleHoo Directory makes this step easy because they show you the addresses of every supplier.

Ask the Manufacturer about the Wholesaler

Characteristically, each and every manufacturer will have a list of all the wholesalers and suppliers they sell their goods to. If the manufacturer of the product has no record of their name, it can be a sign they are not a legitimate company.

Test Processes with a Small Order

By making a short test order, this can be a great way to conclude the skills of a supplier, as well as ensuring they are not a fraudulent company.

Try not to Appear as a Newbie

It doesn't matter if you'll be successfully running your online store 10 years down the road or not, you still need to appear as if you will be.

If you appear like a newbie (i.e. like you don't know what you're talking about), suppliers might take advantage and charge you higher prices than usual. In some instances, they might not even respond to you at all. The best advice to appear professional is to utilize great email templates, do your homework first, and also make sure you are asking plenty of relevant questions. If you do these this you'll get the respect you want, and you might gain the best deals from the best suppliers, too. That's the goal.

Competitor's Suppliers - Who They Use

A good way of finding reliable suppliers is by locating your competitor's to see who they use. You can identify other dropshipping resellers by searching on the internet. If the company only has one location listed on the "Contact Us" page, it is more than likely a dropshipping business. They might even highlight their most successful brands.

So, if they've omitted highlighting any brands, then just scroll through any products that they are offering. Write down any names of the brands on the products you wish to sell.

Asking Suppliers Lots of Questions

After you have identified possible suppliers (as previously mentioned), you need to reach out to them to ask if they perform dropshipping. Not all suppliers are willing to do this. Some suppliers might be awkward to contact, so plan on sending plenty of emails and making routine phone calls until you have reached the correct person.

Once you have done this, ask them the following questions:

What is the lead time for them to ship once you've placed an order with them?

What shipping systems do they provide? For example, do they ship overnight, or internationally as a standard?

Are there warranties on their products? If a product is found to be defective, what do they have in place for replacing it?

What quality control systems do they use to make sure batches of products are reliable?

Do they post minimum recommended advertised prices? Preferably, they would do this, and if they don't, then other dropshipping companies might lower their rates too low for you to compete with them.

Do they charge monthly or annual fees? If they do, then it might be wise to avoid them.

Can you post their product photos on your store's page? If possible, they'll allow you to use their pictures. This saves you time.

WHAT'S ESSENTIAL WHEN WORKING WITH DROPSHIPPING COMPANIES?

In the United States, legal dropshippers won't consider working alongside you unless you have a legitimate business established, and have an EIN, or an Employer Identification Number. This EIN number is the social security number for your business, and, depending on if the state where you live charges sales tax or not, you might also need a sales tax ID from the state you live in.

In the United States, forming a legal company structure isn't as complicated as you might imagine, and you can (in some cases) be completed in an hour or two on your State Dept. of Commerce website, or you can use a site similar to Legal Zoom.

Typically, the incorporation of your business will cost you less than $200, and once your company is officially established with your state, then requesting your EIN number from the IRS is a straightforward process.

It is **vital** you spend some time to suitably investigate what sort of business structure is best suited for you. You'll need to study this at length, and if you are unsure, it is advised that you consult with a professional such as an accountant or an attorney who can assist.

Create a Personal Account with Your Supplier

Some suppliers require you to complete an application form (in case of credit), or you might have to call or go online to set up your account. They will more-than-likely demand a copy of your reseller's certificate, business licenses, and other documentation. It is for this reason you need to create your business, first.

It is crucial for payment methods to be discussed. You can pay in advance or pay on terms once you have proved yourself. When you pay upfront, you are paying at the same time as orders are placed. With paying via terms, you will pay all of your purchased orders at a later date, and, more often than not, this is at the end of the month.

Because you are just starting out, most suppliers might only agree to work with you once you pay upfront, which is generally the case. Once you've established your trustworthiness, they might consider changing their billing options with your business.

Types of Fees that Dropshipping Companies Charge

The potential fees can be encountered with drop shippers:

Per Order Fees -

It's customary for dropshippers to charge per order fees to cover their expenses that are involved in the packaging and shipping of a product. These fees can range from $2 to the $5 range, and they can be much higher for any items that are awfully large or problematic to process.

Monthly Fees -

Some dropshippers might attempt to charge you ongoing monthly fees for nothing more than the privilege of doing business with them.

Much of the time, this indicates poor quality and can mean a "fake" dropshipper. So, do your homework, first. Limited numbers of legitimate dropshipping wholesalers will ask you to pay a monthly fee.

Minimum Purchases -

Some dropshippers will more-than-likely require a minimum purchase size for your first order, or on a monthly basis. If your sales don't meet these sales thresholds, they might charge you a fee. This, they'll do to filter out business owners who are non-serious, and who are likely to be more trouble than they are worth.

A GREAT DROPSHIPPING SUPPLIER

Not every dropshipper is good at what they do. Nevertheless, there are a few ways to finding the best in a big, vast bunch. Before discussing how to locate your dropshipper, we'll take a quick look at what high-value suppliers actually look like.

Helpful and Experienced Sales Reps

One thing to look for in good dropshipping suppliers are excellent sales reps. You need to know that you can call them and get your questions answered thoroughly and as completely as possible. They will also know how to handle any issues you might have.

No one is perfect, and some questions can't be answered right away. Good staff should be willing to find out the answers for you and get back to you promptly with their solutions.

Huge Pre-Order Fees

Generally, dropshippers will charge "pre-order" fees. These fees you need to pay each time you place orders with them. It makes sense from their side, because they need to take extra time and resources in packing and shipping your orders to your customers.

Conversely, occasionally dropshippers take advantage and charge shamefully-high fees. These might range anywhere from $2 to $10. Although this might seem high, it does depend on the profit margins that you can make on your products. Do your homework and do the math to see if you can still make a decent profit when dealing with high fees. If this isn't the case, keep looking.

Quick Shipments

If a supplier is taking more than 24 hours to ship items, they will not be a good match for your business. Dropshipping is an excessively competitive market and there is little (or no room) for lengthy shipping processes. The competition will simply beat you if your shipments take too long.

On the other hand, if you find suppliers who can ship in the least amount of time, you can gain a competitive edge. To see how good dropshipping companies perform, it is good to place a test order before you make your final choice, and see which ones come out on top.

Lower Returns Means a Quality Product

So, selling a high-quality product means:

- High customer satisfaction
- Better and increased word-of-mouth referrals

- Less product returns
- Higher-rated product reviews

The benefits above mean more profit in the long-run for your business. More than you would ever obtain from selling at high-margins with low-quality products.

Investment in Technology

The latest technology in automation, efficiency, and scalability is going to be increasingly important as your dropshipping empire grows. Although not necessary right at the start, you'll need to try and choose suppliers with this long-term goal in mind.

Signs that a good dropshipper has invested in modern technology include:

- An up-to-date website with full product descriptions
- Inventory data feeds which can automatically update your product listings on your store
- Options in place to order and cancel orders on their website or via email

Obviously, not all dropshipping companies will have these advanced features, and they shouldn't necessarily be counted out just because they don't have an attractive website. Just keep these things in the back of your mind during your search.

Branded Products

Sometimes, selling brand-name products is probably a bad idea. This is correct for beginners, especially.

Nevertheless, as you progress as a dropshipping company owner, this might be a category you wish to tackle. If you eventually think you want to sell branded products, this is a factor you should consider when you are looking at choosing a supplier. But, the competition will probably be fierce from the get-go.

CHOOSING THE BEST-SELLING PRODUCTS

ONCE YOU'VE FOUND A GOOD SUPPLIER, YOU NEED TO GO through their product pages to see what items you wish to sell. In an ideal world, you'll want to sell products which are in high demand.

Here you can use some unique techniques to estimate a product's popularity:

Market Research

Doing this, you can find the need for your potential product by using the *Google Keyword Tool*. This tool quickly provides data on the numbers of persons who are searching for a term. As an example, if you wish to sell *sweaters with cats*, you would check how many individuals have searched for that term.

On eBay, Turn to the Completed Listings Page

Go to "advanced search" and check the "completed listings" box. Once you enter your keywords and the category, you can then scroll through the pages of listings and search for items which are selling 60% or more. These product items are usually highly popular.

HOW TO FIND THE BEST DROPSHIPPING PRODUCTS

Dropshipping offers e-commerce business entrepreneurs lots of freedom; however, there are some key factors you'll need to take into contemplation when sourcing your products for your store's inventory. Once you come to understand the varying types of products which can be perfect for your dropshipping store, you'll be way ahead of your competition, and you'll be in a position to start making real sales.

Dropshipping Businesses & Trending Products

Currently, trending products are great options for a dropshipping business inventory. If you can manage to source any trending products for your store before they hit the commercial mainstream, you can take advantage of low marketing fees and establish your store as a frontrunner in that field.

If you have a lot of interest in locating products which are trending, or products which are more than likely to be popular in the near future, you should check out the following online resources:

Kickstarter.com—Wish.com—Wanelo.com—Google Trends

Check through these resources, making a note if you find any products which are trending. Then note down which might be suitable for your store's inventory.

If you have decided on trending products for your online dropshipping store's inventory, spend some time thinking about how you will market your products to your audience.

Finding a Niche

When you're targeting a particular niche with your dropshipping store, it can be a boundless way in helping your dropshipping store to grow and generate good revenue. Use the popular *Google Trends* to do some in-depth research into niches which have a high potential. These will be great niches for your high-quality dropshipping products.

You can have actually lower competition if you run a niche dropshipping store. This happens because you come to target a smaller audience. This means all of your marketing labors become much cheaper. This is true if you're contemplating using Google AdWords or Facebook advertising.

It will also be more natural to rank your online store on search engines when running a niche dropshipping store. This is good news for your long-term business growth. It's vital to know that starting your dropshipping store career in a specific niche doesn't mean that you can't expand into other, more diverse areas later on. Once you've concreted your store as a leader within that specific niche, you can attempt to add related products which you think your customers might be interested in. This will allow your business to branch out and target new customers, too.

Always Specialize in One Niche First, Then Scale Up

Starting out with a large inventory of products will only complicate everything. You'll have to deal with more inventory, extra product listings (on eBay, Amazon, a website, and/or Shopify, as examples). You will also be faced with more competition, and more suppliers to deal with, too.

Start small and hash out any issues with one niche area first, then you can scale up when you feel more comfortable with what you're doing. You need to feel in control, so learning what to do in one niche first will give you the confidence you need to expand later on.

Browse Other Stores and See What to Sell Online

Walmart's founder, Sam Walton, was arrested back in the 1980s for crawling through stores on his hands and knees. He told a close friend he measured all the spaces between the product shelves to conclude how his opponents showed their products.

At that time, Walmart was making $400m plus in their sales. Walton wasn't content and knew there was more he could earn if he mastered the same approaches his competitors used.

When browsing other stores, take a look at their offerings, their best-selling lists, and their promoted products. There are a great number of online stores which have remarkable amounts of data and employ whole departments in organizing their sales and selecting their products. Use this information to your overall benefit. Spend a lot of time browsing, and be sure to browse often. It can help you find some great dropshipping ideas.

Here are online stores and resources you should review regularly:

Amazon Best Sellers—eBay Daily Deals—Lazada Top

Sellers—LightInTheBox Top Sellers List—Oberle's List of What to Sell Online

Social Shopping Sites for Dropshipping Ideas

Polyvore has over 100 million products, and *Wanelo* has 30 million. If you add in *Fancy, Pinterest,* and also *Instagram,* this equates to a significant number of products from all around the globe which can be easily incorporated by popularity, category, and more.

A lot of people might often overlook these sites while doing their research. They do turn out to be valuable resources for drawing perceptions of which kinds of products are trending on the internet from each day to the next.

It is highly recommended that you set up an account with each of these websites. You can subscribe to diverse categories and lists, and follow what individuals like the most, and add those things onto your list to help you. When you continually surround yourself with inspiration, you'll rapidly come up with plenty of dropshipping ideas that have a high profit-generating potential.

Dropshipping Ideas from Friends

A good tip is to review some *Google Trends* products before you have coffee with friends and ask what they think of those product ideas. Make sure not to limit yourself to your own personal demographics, either. Speak with friends from all age groups and backgrounds to get a broad variety of dropshipping ideas, and a more extensive range of assessments of what you can sell online. There is a good chance you'll end up with dropshipping ideas you have not even considered. These might make your e-commerce dropshipping store so much better.

Additional Ideas of What to Sell Online

Spend time looking around your home, workplace, and around your community that you visit often. Are there products you or friends can't live without? Which products go a long way to make your life easier? Is there anything hard to find in the supermarket, or at local stores? Any answers to these questions can hold the keys to products you want to sell online, and that can essentially return a profit for you, too.

A thought to consider: Howard Schultz dreamt up his coffee shop idea while visiting Italy. He later called it Starbucks. There are plenty of dropshipping ideas which can come to mind when traveling. And it's just as equally possible to spot them in everyday life. Begin with your daily life and use it as its own databank for producing dropshipping ideas. Remain alert and spot those golden opportunities, and once you embrace this mindset, you'll begin seeing hundreds of products and dropshipping ideas, each and every day.

When you are active with your idea creation, you can quickly come up with an extensive list of the best dropshipping products for your store. Be observant, and carry a notebook to take notes... and remember, the most important part is to write everything down.

Avoid Certain Sites for Dropshipping Ideas

When finalizing your list of products to sell online, it is suggested you don't look at sites like *SpringWise* or *TrendHunter*. These are great sites, but they are better-suited for other purposes.

In other words, the products featured might be difficult to obtain for decent dropshipping intentions. They will provide useful dropshipping ideas. However, they might not necessarily be a right match for your store, alternatively, the items listed might already have fierce competition.

WHERE TO SELL

WITH PRODUCTS SELECTED, YOUR SUPPLIERS LOCKED INTO place, and your company being legal, now it's now time to start your selling processes! At this point, you need to decide on how to present your products to prospective customers. Several sales options are currently available, but, more-than-likely, you will choose one: your own online store, eBay, or Amazon.

eBay Dropshipping

Being the world's largest online auction site for physical goods, eBay is a site many people are familiar with. Here are a few reasons you might wish to consider or avoid eBay for your dropshipping:

eBay Selling Pros: Easy to Start

With eBay, you can instantly dive in and start creating listings of your products. Create your account, add the listings, and you are in business.

Accessing a Larger Audience

When selling on eBay, you have greater access to many online buyers who frequent the site. There are potentially millions of shoppers who will see your listings, and the fairly robust and active market helps to ensure you get a respectable price for all of your products.

Lower Marketing Levels

There is no need to worry about marketing, SEO, or paying to have re-directed traffic. As you are able to piggyback off the eBay platform, this can save you time, because this marketing is one of the most substantial challenges that is associated with launching any business.

eBay Selling Cons: Listing Fees

The major downside to selling on eBay is the fees you'll need to pay. The most notable being a success fee which can be up to 10% (or higher) of the sale price you have placed on your items. While you are dropshipping, margins need to be super-tight and this might cut into any significant percentage of your profits.

Constant Monitoring and Relisting

eBay is an auction (styled) marketplace. You will need to repeatedly monitor and relist the products you are selling, unless you choose the "buy it now" feature that's available. You can find some tools which help automate this process, nonetheless, it's still very straightforward.

The Sales Platform Can't Be Customized

eBay has templates, and your product listings need to follow these rules. This means you can't create professional pages which add value for your items.

No Long-Term Loyalty from Customers

It might be possible to have some repeat eBay customers; nonetheless, most won't buy from you again, unless it's a product that needs restocking. Any goodwill you could build up through excellent service will, in most cases, be lost.

The structure of the marketplace is created to serve itself, and eBay doesn't want to place their focus on "you," the merchant, they only focus on their products. You are significantly restricted in how you can communicate with your customers, how you are able to brand yourself, and any design choice regarding your store within this platform.

No Assets Being Built

When you create an online store which generates traffic and brings repeat custom, you naturally build a real business which has value, and that is something you can sell to others at a later date. When you sell goods on eBay, you are not making a long-lasting brand, or a web property which has any substance which could be sold in the future.

Dropshipping on Amazon

Amazon does stock and sell some items, although (like eBay), many of the listed products are sold by third-party merchants using Amazon's website. Similarly to eBay, Amazon facilitates the sale, and resolves any problems that arise.

The Pros of Selling on Amazon

Advantages of selling on Amazon are very similar to the ones mentioned for eBay. It's very easy to start, you have immediate access to a wide-ranging audience, and you have little need to worry about marketing or major SEO (search engine optimization). I would always make sure the title of your product/s includes common keywords, however.

Amazon will also offer its own fulfillment warehouses (FBA), which allows you to complement any dropshipped items with your own products, all without dealing with packing, shipping, or warehousing.

The Cons of Selling on Amazon: Listing Fees

Likewise, as with eBay, you'll pay Amazon for access to their extensive network of buyers. Amazon's commission varies by product type, and it is usually in the 10% to 15% price range. If you're working with small dropshipping margins, this could take a hefty slice out of your profits.

Exposure to Sales Data

Amazon sees all of your sales data, from the items which sell the best, to how many products you're selling, overall. Previously, Amazon has been accused of making full use of this data to identify the best selling opportunities, and to strengthen its own position in the niche. This could ultimately push out other merchants, and makes for fiercer competition.

Lack of Long-Term Customer Connection

Just like eBay, and maybe even worse, it's highly unlikely you'll grow a long-term relationship with any of your customers. That's unless you are selling restock-type products. Amazon exists to help themselves. It's in their best interest to focus on products and customers, rather than the sellers. You should be equipped to be limited about how you can brand your business, display products, and communicate with any of your customers.

No Customization

Like eBay, you are highly restricted regarding customization. Everything is under Amazon's control. Branding, UI, marketing, and everything else, really.

Dropshipping with Your Own Online Store

There is an alternative to selling through third-party sites like Amazon and eBay. Establishing your own online store to sell products is the method which attracts the most people who are interested in building a successful dropshipping business. But, we need to take an in-depth approach to cover this.

Having Your Own Store: The Pros of Selling with Your Own Store

More Overall Control

With your own online e-commerce store you choose the shopping environment that's best suited to selling your products, all while adding the all-important value to your customers' experience by way of price and other incorporations. You are free to customize the look and layout, and create custom product pages which are optimized to best notify your customers about your products.

More Comfortable Design

Actually, building and owning an e-commerce store is easy, especially with platforms like Shopify. Simply choose a store design (out of hundreds of options) and make any customizations you want. Next, add your products and link to a payment gateway, and you are ready to go. If your e-commerce store isn't anything complicated, you can be up and running within one day. Wow.

Ready for Mobile

eBay and Amazon can be a pain via mobile shopping. If you decide to build your online e-commerce store with popular, hosted, e-commerce platforms, then your site will be more responsive. This means it will look good and operate on any mobile device. This is more and more imperative these days, because approximately 60% of online purchases are made via mobile devices.

Some online store platforms (such as Shopify) will let you manage your whole business from your mobile device. This is predominantly appealing to dropshipping company owners who often like running their business on-the-go, or even from a warm beach somewhere. Sounds inviting.

No Third-Party Fees

On your own site, you don't have to pay 10% to 15% of each sale you make (to platforms like eBay or Amazon). This can have a significant impact on your overall profit margin.

Building a Real Business

With this, you will be creating a long-term business with a distinctive feel. It might be regarded for expertise and have many repeat customers. Most prominently, you'll be constructing a business which has equity. This is far easier when selling a company that's proven itself on a self-sufficient, well-maintained website.

The Cons of Selling on Your Own Store

Lower Amounts of Free Traffic

With your own e-commerce site, you are responsible for the generating of traffic through marketing, SEO, and any other paid advertising you use. There are many more costs involved here. This, via funding added in to the cause, or any time that is invested by you. Additionally, you will need to be ready to spend cash in a long-term campaign with which to promote your new store.

11

AVOIDING COMMON DROPSHIPPING MISTAKES

Once you've decided to start dropshipping, you need to ensure you have a solid business strategy in place, right from the start. This means you should be ready to avoid all these common mistakes. Let's take a look at these now.

Expecting Products to Sell

As previously mentioned, dropshipping (by design) places you in a competitive situation, for the reason that others are marketing precisely the same thing you are. It's all too laid-back an idea to contemplate that you'll be setting up dropshipping for your online store and that you will have an instant money-making scheme on your hands.

The exact opposite is true. With dropshipping, you need to place all of the time which you save on shipping and fulfillment into your marketing and SEO campaigns and efforts.

These are the elements which will drive customer traffic toward your store, and make you sales when you're a merchant who uses dropshipping. Since you can't control any side of the fulfillment or packaging/posting with dropshipping, you should always put a priority-focus on high-quality customer service. Additionally, you should make sure you give customers a positive and lasting experience in the areas of the purchasing process you find that you can control.

Reliant On One Supplier or Not Having a Backup Plan

If you only turn to one supplier without having any back-up, you're leaving yourself with logistical issues further down the line. What happens if your supplier raises prices to where you can't afford them? Or what if they go out of business? They might just decide to no longer work with you anymore, which can happen, too. I'm not big on "what ifs" in my personal life, but professionally I am, to stay ahead of the game.

Even on a less severe note, a supplier could be just out of stock on a product and be unable to answer when they'll have that stock in again, It's crucial to always have a backup supplier that you can turn to if your primary supplier doesn't work out for any particular reason/s.

Each time you start to work with a new supplier, you need to make sure that they perform, and you should place test orders to be sure. Once you get the order, examine it, and consider the packaging, the shipment time, and so on while making sure everything is the quality in which you expect. It is advisable to place test orders on a regular basis, although not detrimental. Fulfillment is as crucially important to any online business though, and you need to catch any dips in quality before they start becoming real issues.

Stressing Over Shipping Rates

Shipping rates can be an aggravation, even when you ship all your products from one location. If you ship from several warehouses or dropship via multiple suppliers, it can be a bit of a nightmare. What if an order draws on two different warehouses, or three different suppliers? Eeek!

Take a step back and take a good look at the bigger picture. What is it you aim to achieve? Is it better shipping rates? Or more sales and content customers who want repeat business? If you waste energy over shipping rates on every single order, that's energy not devoted to: creating better customer shopping experiences, increasing the size of your store, your marketing, and everything else you should focus on in terms of customer happiness, overall.

Take a look at previous orders, and use these to calculate flat shipping rates, or maybe tiered rates based on cart value. Will it slice into your profit margins? Yes, on some fulfilled orders. The difference is, you will come out ahead of others, and if you've set your rates correctly, shipping costs should be even cheaper, over time.

It has also been shown that flat prices and free shipping increases conversion rates. One primary reason that customers abandon their shopping carts is due to high shipping costs. Flat shipping fees remove confusion and superficially "hidden" fees which show up at checkout.

12

HOW TO RUN YOUR DROPSHIPPING COMPANY

Required Commitment

LIKE OTHER BUSINESS TYPES, SUCCESSFUL BUILDING OF A dropshipping business takes significant commitment and a long-term outlook. If you're hoping for a six-figure income from just six weeks of part-time work, then you will be very-much disappointed.

When you approach your business with accurate anticipations about your investment required, and add-in your overall profitability, you will be much less likely to be discouraged and quit. When beginning a dropshipping business, you will need to heavily invest in one of the following two currencies: either time, or money. Let's cover these now.

Investing Time

Investing "sweat" toward building your business is the suggested tactic, particularly for first-time dropshipping entrepreneurs. I support this slant over spending a considerable sum of money for many reasons:

1. You'll come to learn how your company functions inside and out, which is crucial for handling others as your company grows and scales upward.
2. You'll intimately know what your customers want, and the market, and this allows you to make healthier decisions.
3. You will develop many new skills that will make you a better and more-confident entrepreneur.

Most people can't just quit their job to spend six months building their new online e-commerce store. It might be a bit more perplexing, but it's certainly conceivable to start with dropshipping, even while still being employed in a 9 to 5 position.

Supposing you set suitable expectations concerning customer service and fulfillment times for your customers, then that would be a great start. As you begin to increase, you can then changeover into working full-time on your company as your cash-flow and profitability allow for it.

All companies and entrepreneurs are highly unique, although it's possible to earn $1,000 to $2,000 as a monthly income stream within a 12-month working period, or more, while spending roughly 10 to 15 hours per week constructing your business.

If you have the option of working on your business full-time, it's also the best option to increase profit potential and your chances of success. Concentrating your efforts on marketing is particularly helpful in the beginning when you are building up momentum.

Based on experience, it typically takes at least 12 months of full-time effort with robust importance on marketing. In truth, this is around the time it takes for dropshipping businesses to substitute a regular full-time income of $50,000 or more.

When your dropshipping company is up and running, preserving it will more-than-likely take expressively less time than a 40-hour-per-week ignition, in contrast to a "normal" career. In fact, a lot of your investment will pay off multitudes by using a dropshipping model that is well thought out.

When you build a business, you're generating more than only an income stream. You are also developing an asset which you can possibly sell in the future. Make sure you contemplate the equity value you're accruing, as well as the cash flow generated when looking at your actual return.

Investing Your Money

It's conceivable to produce and grow a dropshipping company by spending a significant amount of money, but then again, I recommend against doing this.

In the initial stages, it's vital to have somebody who is intensely invested in the triumph of the company and creating it from the ground up. Deprived of knowledge on how your business works at each level, you could be at the mercy of programmers, website developers, and marketers who'll quickly gobble up any profits you manage to generate. You don't have to do all the work yourself, although, it is recommended that you are the primary driving force at the start of your venture.

In the beginning, you will need a small cash cushion of around $1,000 to get you're a business launched and fully operational. This would be required for minor operating expenses (web hosting, internet, and suppliers) as well as paying any incorporation fees necessary.

Choosing your Business Structure

Note: Business structures and the EIN (Employer Identification Number) information discussed here, are only applicable for entrepreneurs in the United States.

Sole Proprietorship

This is the most natural and most straightforward business arrangement to apply, nonetheless, it also poses no personal liability protection. If your company is issued, all of your personal assets might also be in danger. Filing requirements are negligible, and you only report any business earnings on your own taxes. No additional state or federal business filings are compulsory.

Limited Liability Company (LLC)

An LLC gives improved protection of your personal assets. This is done by founding your business as an unconnected legal body. Although the liability protection isn't foolproof, it provides additional protection, compared with a sole-proprietorship.

You might need to fulfill supplementary filing necessities, and you will have to pay both incorporation and open-ended fees.

C Corporation

Most substantial corporations are created as C corporations, which; when suitably done, will provide the most liability protection. They are more expensive to set up and incorporate, and are subject to double-taxation, as any income doesn't pass straight to shareholders.

What is the best structure to choose? Many small entrepreneurs are inclined to go with one, either a sole proprietorship or an LLC. LLC for dropshipping businesses can offer the best trade-off concerning liability protection, and a distance from personal finances and costs.

Requesting an EIN Number

All businesses need an employer identification number (EIN), as required by The IRS. This acts as a Social Security number for your business and is required to file taxes, apply for wholesale dropshipping accounts, open a bank account, and almost anything else that's related to your business.

Getting Your Finances in Order

A frequent mistake entrepreneurs make when starting up, is merging personal and business finances. This will cause confusion and makes accounting difficult, it can also lead to the personal assumption of business liabilities (which is a huge red flag to the IRS).

Keep business and personal finances detached as much as possible; this is detrimental. The best way is by opening new accounts in your business name.

You'll want a new:

Business Checking Account

All of your business finances should go through one primary checking account. All business revenue ought to be deposited into it, and all expenses withdrawn from it, too. This makes accounting much more comfortable and more accessible.

PayPal Account

If you are going to accept PayPal payments, you will want a separate account for your business. Keep your personal one for personal use only.

Credit Card

You should possess a business credit card which is used for all business expenses and for dropshipping inventory purchases only. Since you'll be buying a lot of merchandise from your suppliers, you can mount up some serious rewards with the right "reward" cards.

Collecting Sales Tax

Collect sales tax if both of the following are true:

- The state where you operate collects sales tax

AND

- An order is placed by someone living in your state

For orders placed from other states, even if these states charge a separate sales tax, you won't need to collect any tax at present. Get advice from an accountant if you're unsure.

If your state charges sales tax, be prepared that you need to collect it on the number of orders from your customers who live in your home state.

Contacting your state's *Department of Commerce* to register as a retailer is the best way to find out how frequently you need to submit your tax that you collect.

Business Licenses - Local

Most cities require businesses to get a business license which needs renewing on a regular basis. But, this requirement might differ for dropshipping companies, a lot of which will likely be operated from a home office. You'll need to check into your local laws and regulations to find out if anything is required.

Incorporating Outside of the US

It can be very complicated, although it is possible for international dealers to incorporate a business within the United States. This gives them access to US-based dropshippers and potential customers, too.

The merchant would need to come to the US to complete any necessary paperwork, or have a trusted business partner in the US who can act on their behalf to set everything up.

Toll-Free Numbers:

Any business that has a toll-free number looks more legitimate for customers who wish to call and lodge complaints, or ask questions. Some providers even allow the linking of this number to your cell phone.

If you don't wish to use your home address for your business address, then you can get a mailbox from the post office or a UPS store.

List your Products for Sale:

Correct pricing is important. You don't want a high price, or you could lose customers to your competitors. However, if your prices are too low, there isn't much chance for profit.

Always allow for how much you will pay your supplier when setting your sale price, and don't forget that your supplier will also charge you for shipping. Explicitly inform your customers about shipping and return policies in your listings. Your customers need to know this information, upfront.

Online selling platforms such as eBay and Amazon require you to identify where products are located.

Make the Purchase when You Get a Sale:

As a merchant using dropshipping, you will wait for your customer to make an order. Once they do, you order from your supplier. Make sure there is no delay, since this only causes a delay to your customer.

Pay the Supplier Using your Rewards Credit Card:

Once you receive a tracking number, hold onto it and track the product so that you know when it has arrived.

Notify Your Customers When Their Product Ships:

You should stay in continual contact with your customer after they purchase a product. Send a follow-up email informing them when their product was shipped. Also, provide any contact information so they can contact you if they have a problem.

Problem Troubleshooting:

Many issues will arise in the dropshipping business. Example: your supplier might not be dependable and could send an order too late. Or the product isn't packaged securely, and it breaks.

You can increase protection by having several suppliers for the majority of your products. This way, you will always have a fallback option if your primary supplier isn't able to deliver. This could be professionally, or because they are "out of stock."

When a product becomes "sold out," you can provide your customer with an upgraded product for free, rather than canceling the order. Or send them a freebie for waiting longer. This works really well. Remember to stay in continual contact with your suppliers here. You need a good working relationship with them so they can help remedy any problems.

Are There Restocking Fees?

It's true that some suppliers may charge you a fee for restocking, if you do get any returns, that is. I don't recommend passing on this fee to your customer. Yes, losses will occur, but, it will be worth it in the long run to take it on, because you'll ultimately be able to retain customers who could have gone elsewhere. A loyal customer following is always the wanted outcome, for sure.

Defective Items

Now, whether you like it or not, most suppliers will charge a fee to return items, even if they're deemed "defective." Hopefully, it doesn't happen to you, but you should be prepared, just in case.

The most important things to note can be summed up by two main points. Firstly, don't pass this fee on to your customer. We want to build loyalty, and the loss here is worth it, long-term. Secondly, if a customer does receive a "defective" item, send them a replacement, free of charge, and don't make them send the old one back. This kind of trust denoted by you as the seller (or business) will gain the admiration of your customer, and awesome customer service is pivotal for long-term success. They might even recommend you to friends or colleagues.

What to Do When a Supplier Messes Up an Order

Sometimes, the supplier will make a mistake. Yes, it happens. They might post the wrong item to the right person, or vice versa.

Here, it's important for you to contact the supplier and tell them exactly what happened. A great supplier will always reimburse you for their mistake. Send the supplier your explanation via email, rather than by telephone, then, you'll have a record should legal action ever be required. Usually, nothing drastic will come to fruition, but if it does, you'll be fully prepared.

If it's a huge mistake and your supplier refuses to reimburse your account, you can file a chargeback against them, via your credit card company. Additionally, you can also send them a detailed letter stating that you will take legal action if they continue to refuse your refund. This is also a great plan of action.

If you don't want to bring out the "artillery" then you can suffer the loss and find a new, more-reliable supplier. A great relationship with a supplier is extremely important for both parties involved.

Managing Inventory across Multiple Suppliers

One of the biggest headaches of dropshipping using a variety of suppliers (which is thoroughly recommended) is dealing with a huge inventory. In fact, inventory management means that you'll need to be checking your suppliers' websites, every time you go to place an order. Of course, this can be time-consuming, so using software is a great idea, if you can. You should consider investing in software to help take the pressure off some of your workload, and also because it will prevent backorders, too.

Dealing With Out-of-Stock Orders & Fulfilling Dropship Orders

Sometimes, you'll get an order for an item that's actually out of stock. When this happens, a great tip is to put the product on "back-order" and explain the situation to the buyer, as soon as you can. Send them an immediate email to let them know you can't adhere to the order, and give them the options. They can either choose to get a refund, or they can wait for the item to arrive. Make sure you tell them "when" and "why" this is happening. You want to create trust. Send them a free "something" for their trouble. All customers love that. Low-cost, but showing that you care about their wait time.

Customer Support & All You Need to Know

Customer support plays a significant role in your dropshipping company, and its subsequent success or failure. Having an excellent customer service plan and auctioning will help carry your company to the top, while poor customer service can cost you money and ultimately put an end to your business.

Due to fierce competition in the overall dropshipping industry, customer service can be your company's competitive edge.

Here is a concise overview of the varying types of customer support you can use for success:

Email - Email will be your primary support channel. If people have any questions, this is the first place most of them will go to voice their concerns.

It is recommended to create an email for your website called "your-businessname@yoursite.com." Or, if you wish not to associate your brand with your personal information, choose "support@your-site.com."

Phone - Phone support can be a part of your support strategy. However, through experience, it has been found not to be the most effective form of service. It can be costly too, in terms of time and money. You can, however, learn much about customers and their quibbles and wants by speaking to them over the phone.

If you plan on including phone support, consider the creation of a free Google Voice number. This is a separate number which you can route back to your own telephone number and also includes a different voicemail.

This way, there is no need to hand out your personal number, and you can keep track of "business only" calls.

Live Chat - Live chat has become the go-to method of support in recent times. It makes sense because many people don't want to wait for responses, and many have no desire to get on the phone. However, live chat can only apply if you have your own website.

The benefits of live chat include higher chances of catching customer complaints and issues. You can check out free live chat apps like Formilla.

Social Media - For similar reasons that live chat continues thriving, social media has now become the go-to option for customer support. This includes questions and concerns.

If you do have a presence on social media (which is highly suggested), it's imperative to respond to all comments and messages from customers and followers. If you don't, it makes you look like you are not bothered with them, and gives your competition the advantage.

Help Desks – It might not be something you need to think of in the beginning, but eventually, if you grow, you need a system to keep track of customer questions. This is where help desk software comes into play.

A basic help desk is a digital hub for all customer questions, comments, and shipping concerns.

Groove is one of the best help desk options you can find to help with this, with HelpScout coming a close second.

Virtual Assistants – When you get to a certain size of expansion, sooner or later you have to make a decision. Do you continue spending half the day on customer service, or can you afford to hire someone to manage this so you can focus on further growing your business? This is where hiring a virtual assistant (VA) shows its real benefits.

VAs are a great option because you can hire them on a contract basis.

This means no employment paperwork and no worries of firing some-one, either. There are platforms like Upwork that are suited well to this. Your employee/s can also work from anywhere in the world as. long as they have an internet connection.

13

ALL ABOUT ORDERS

WHAT TO DO WHEN YOU RECEIVE CUSTOMER ORDERS?

THE ANSWER TO THIS WILL DEPEND ON HOW MANY SUPPLIERS you have for your products, where they are located, your cost, and their availability. It also depends if you wish to automate your drop-ship fulfilment processes or handle them personally. Regardless of the methods you choose, you'll need all of your automation emails to include the following:

- A purchase order (PO) number if you are using them
- The product title or description
- The SKU number of your products
- The number of products ordered
- All shipping information for your customers - this will be the name and address of where your products are being delivered.

Send All of your Orders to the Preferred Supplier via Email, Automatically

The first and best method I'll talk about is the automation of your ordering process, which will include directing emails to your preferred supplier for each product.

By "preferred supplier," I mean the one who offers the best deals and the best product. Otherwise, you can route your orders to the supplier you wish to develop a much closer working relationship with. One way to automate this process is by just adding your supplier's email address as a recipient for every order you receive.

Sending Orders to Suppliers Based on Geographical Location

This might be a little more challenging to automate, although, sending customer orders to suppliers who are based closer to their geographic location is an excellent idea, especially if you need your orders to reach your customers as fast as possible.

A good example being, if you receive an order from the west coast of the US, you might want a local supplier in that area to process your request. This will lead to quicker shipping times, compared to a supplier who is based further afield.

Availability for Shipping Orders

You can see that managing inventory from several sources can complicate the process. You might need to send your orders to a supplier (who is less than ideal), purely because none of the others have the inventory in stock. This can be problematic to automate also, but then again, using third-party inventory management software will help with this process.

Shipping Orders Based on your Product Cost

A lower item cost will mean you have more significant profit margins. If you wish to maximize your returns, you should conduct price comparisons for your products with all of your suppliers. You need to calculate which one gives the best prices and highest profits so you can then automate everything to that vendor, keeping the others in the wings, just in case.

Avoiding Fraudulent Dropship Orders

Fraudulent orders are another online store concern you could encounter. Fraud is no fun. Nonetheless, it can be avoided with just a little common sense.

14

COMMON WARNING SIGNS OF FRAUD INCLUDE

Different Billing and Shipping Address

ON MANY OCCASIONS, SCAMMERS WILL USE ANOTHER PERSON'S credit card to pay for items. Consequently, the billing and shipping addresses will not match.

Bear in mind, this can also be an individual who is purchasing a gift or living at a temporary address, so be wary of this, too. To avoid any fraud (and the potential of upsetting your customer) give them a quick call just to be on the safe side.

The most significant red flag you can face is that the billing and shipping addresses are in entirely different countries.

Unlike Names on Billing and Shipping Address

Again, you could come across people who are purchasing a gift for someone. A quick phone call can help to avoid any costly mishaps.

Random or Strange Email Addresses

If you receive an order from b1a2r3f4@aol.com, it could be a sign something is not right with the order.

Expedited Shipping

On most occasions, a fraudulent order comes with express shipping. This would give the crook the chance to receive their item quickly and "vanish" before anyone notices.

Information on Charge-Backs

These charge-backs occur when a customer (or fraudster) notifies their credit card company that something is not right with their order. This could mean they never received their order, it wasn't what they expected, or they don't recognize the charge on their statement.

If you don't manage to resolve this dispute, you might lose money from the transaction by having to give a refund, and you will likely be faced with a fee on top of that, ranging anywhere from $15 to $25.

When these charge-backs happen (and they will), don't panic. On many occasions, these are legitimate concerns. It might mean a child has used their parent's credit card, a customer is unhappy with their order, or the product never arrived. With this said, react quickly! You might only have a couple of days to fix this problem.

The information needed will be any documentation relating to the original order and tracking information, showing delivery. This should include a wholesale packing slip indicating which items you purchased and were shipped. If the charge-back is for a legitimate transaction, you will likely be able to get funds back. The key is providing as much evidence as you can in supporting your order.

When the charge-back is for an order with different billing and shipping addresses, there is a good chance you are going to lose. Very few businesses win these types of charge-back cases, actually. Some payment processors might only provide charge-back protection on any orders which are shipped to the billing address that is associated with the card.

That's why you need to be extra careful with these types of orders.

MARKETING YOUR NEW DROPSHIPPING STORE

OKAY, SO THIS TOPIC IS HUGE. AND, OBVIOUSLY, I CAN'T COVER everything. But, what I will highlight are the most important ones, like getting customer reviews and the use of social media platforms as must-do necessities.

I will delve into some key, basic, marketing strategies, so you can get a gist of what you need to begin with. I would also like to add, that the importance of this section is kind of crucial, especially if you aren't using platforms like Amazon or eBay.

Ready? Great. Okay, so let's begin with the most important marketing tactic, ever!!! Yep, it's customer reviews, hands down.

Customer Reviews

Okay, so let's be clear here. If you rely only on Amazon or eBay, then it's definitely true that customer reviews will either make or break your product's success. Reread that; it's pivotal.

If you see a product and the reviews are awful, you steer clear, don't you? This is the biggest "killer" of the market, actually. Even if your price is lower than your competitors' prices, it makes no difference, because your product will seem worthless with negatively worded or low-starred reviews.

Here are 4 Pivotal Ways to Get Amazing Reviews:

1. Sell An Awesome Product

Pick the best product/s to give to your audience. Great quality and value products are definitely important.

1. Give Your Customers Excellent Service

Reply faster, acknowledge them with great communication, and always be professional.

1. Ship Your Products on Time, or Quicker

Try to beat a customer's expectation. If you say items ship within 4 business days, why not try to ship within 3? They will be impressed.

1. Ask Customers for a Review

Some customers forget or don't even realize they should leave reviews. Send an email or ask on social media. In addition, you can also start giving away free products for unbiased reviews, on the Amazon or eBay marketplaces. In fact, eBooks are great freebies.

Tips for eBay Listing Upgrades

When optimizing your products on eBay during the listing process, make sure you don't forget to add in all the options available to you in the listing upgrades, as you go.

These upgrades might include bold font, extra images, additional subtitles, and more. The more professional you can be here, the more it will make a difference. And, even spelling and picture quality counts. So, make the effort so your sales aren't hampered. If you are going to list, do it with your best text, awesome imagery, an excellent description, and as much detail as possible. Would you want to buy the product? Entice your customers so that they will.

The "Gallery Plus" Upgrade Feature

The "gallery plus" upgrade costs around $0.35. It's $1 to keep, until it's canceled. This shows customers a bigger version of your featured image in the search results. Most buyers click on products based on the image first, so this seems like a great upgrade. Make sure you crop your pictures and have great lighting too. Never use blurry or unprofessional-looking imagery. Remember the old saying, "A picture tells a thousand words."

Social Media Marketing

This tool has become such an integral part of nearly everyone's daily lives. It's great to use it as a way of marketing your products, too. I believe that without social media, it's really hard to promote anything. This is especially true if you're not on Amazon and eBay.

When it comes to marketing on social media, less is always more...

Okay, so here it's important to pick one or two networks that make the most sense, and then you can elaborate your networking and marketing from there. I believe Facebook is a must-have platform, for nearly every business and product you want to sell. With around 1.8 billion active users per month, it's a no-brainer that you would go there to market your products. The brilliance of the platform is that it encompasses nearly every type of demographic of people. These demographics target: gender, country, age group, interests, and more. So, you can actually choose this important information before you promote your page. If you are selling men's shoes as an example, then you can choose your gender and age group to fit. Although, I would still market these to women, because statistically speaking, women are the biggest shoppers. Use common sense with demographics. It's no good marketing athletic shoes women over eighty.

You should market on Facebook and choose 1 or more of these platforms too:

- **Twitter**
- **Pinterest**
- **Instagram**
- **Google+**

Awesome Marketing Tactics: Use Pay-Per-Click (PPC) Advertising

This is a really classic marketing avenue. It's a simple type of exchange, converting money for traffic or clicks.

Types of PPC advertising include: social media, Google Adwords, and adverts (e.g. Outbrain).

The basic idea is to not pay too much for advertising. Start smaller to scope out the market using different strategies, first. The one that performs best can be your top pick. You want to convert this style of advertising to sales, not just get your product or business out there. Take a look around at other successful, well-versed, conversion businesses. What do they do, and how can you better their techniques?

Use Email Marketing

Email has to be the most important marketing tactic you'll ever master, because you can reach so many individuals, more personally.

In fact, this is the BEST reason to have your own website. You can get their address easily, and you can send out new product advertisements, coupons, or information to help sell your products.

Use Mailchimp, ConvertKit, or Aweber. Using automated email campaigns is great when you set them in motion. And, over time, you should see an increase in sales, especially if you are targeting your audience well. Shopify also has a great guide on eCommerce email marketing if you want to learn more on this wide subject.

Use Growth Hacking

"Growth hacking" is the term used for marketing in styles that are inexpensive, very effective, and creative, as well. Use content marketing, guest posts on blogs, and targeted campaigns that are pushed at your unique audience. Sellbrite has a great guide than can teach you more tips and tricks for growth hacking if you'd like to learn more.

Coping with Refunds, Returns & Replacements

Stay in line with these steps to keep your customers happy:

1. First, you'll receive a request for a return or refund.
2. Now, you'll request a return merchandise authorization (RMA) number from your supplier, or suppliers, if there is more than one.
3. Ask the customer to mail back the merchandise to your supplier, making sure that the RMA number is included.
4. The supplier refunds your account for the merchandise.

This refund will be the wholesale cost, not the price the customer paid.

5. Once your refund is issued, you'll then refund your customer the price they paid for the product/s.

Always be aware of your supplier's return policy as stated in their guidelines. If they have a nice window for refund, then you can pass a great window to your customers, too. Make sure you know this, otherwise you will be refunding at a loss, and that doesn't make any cents (or sense), pardon the pun.

THINGS TO DO FOR EXTRA SUCCESS

With a lot of dropshipping areas in your business being automated, you should have more time with which to focus on marketing. While fine-tuning a website, designing logos, and creating graphics can be plenty of fun, it is your marketing that is your real money maker.

You need to spend some time learning how to master ads, increase your traffic, and in converting your online store's presence by sending visitors to it.

Ads and search engine optimization might help to increase traffic which is driven to your store, bearing in mind, that many e-commerce stores have conversion rates of 1-2%. This equates to less than 100 visitors on your site, per day, and means there is a high chance you won't be making any sales.

The higher amounts of traffic that visit your store means that; the more likely it will be that you can convert the sale. A lot of online stores focus on ads because they can provide instant gratification and have the capability to drive more sales in a shorter period of time.

Nevertheless, SEO helps a great deal in driving the long-term sales by helping you rank higher in search engines. Blog content and the optimization of product pages on your website will help to build a growing audience. Use the minimal advertisement spend, and keep your procurement costs low, but purposeful.

Does your website appear presentable from your customer's point of view? And, are you missing any images on your homepage? There are a lot of things which need to be considered to ensure your online store is optimized, both correctly and efficiently.

Test the Market & Other Factors

When first starting out, you are best to test a market by use of drop-shipping. Do this before you commit to purchasing a significant amount of inventory, and buying in bulk. Once you understand a little more about how the market works, this will include how much product you can realistically expect to sell, then you can decide if the market supports your dropshipping.

Create Those Amazing Offers

An essential dropshipping tip is creating compelling offers. You should make sure you aren't the storeowner who fails to include product sales or item bundles. If none of your products show as being in "a sale," people might lack any motivation in which to purchase your product. But, if you present the right products in the right deals, you stand more chance to convert them into sales.

Deal bundles also work really well. When you creating a bundle deal, you should focus on selling more of the same product. A great example being, if you are selling hair extensions, your bundle should include more hair extensions as additional "worms" to "hook" your customers. People love a bundle.

If you find people love the product, they'll desire to have more of it. The hardest part is to convince your customer to whip out their credit card to make the purchase. We want them to need it "Now!"

Don't Under-Price Any Products

When you dropship products from AliExpress or Oberlo, supply will allow you to keep product costs in a lower range. The cost of the goods is typically close to a wholesale price, and this will enable you to sell your products at market value and still make a profit.

The main goal of a dropshipping business is profitability. If you sell a $5 product (cost), you should be charging in the region of around $19.99 for it. You also need to factor in the cost of your marketing, and business expenses, and the thoughts of eventually hiring a team.

If you find other brands are undercutting your prices, you shouldn't follow suit and undermine yours. As long as you have fair prices and are within market value, you should be able to maintain a price point that is still quite profitable. You should also aim to increase your average order values so you can make higher profits from each order. Create a strategy that will help you make more money, overall.

Remove Bad Suppliers

While the majority of suppliers are pleasant to work with, and offer reliable, excellent products, it sometimes occurs that a bad apple, or two, appears.

If you spot suppliers who don't use the required shipping delivery methods you initially chose, or they consistently ship faulty products, you can quickly remove the products you purchase from them from your store.

In truth, this scenario isn't overly-familiar. A good number of suppliers know by offering a quality service that you'll continue using them in the future.

Automating Your Business

Using fantastic tools like Oberlo, means that a variety of aspects of your business will be automated. But, if you have a 9 to 5 job, or are looking to create a more passive way to make income, this becomes key.

Go to the Oberlo pages and read the blogs and information given there. It will open your eyes to new ways of doing automated business, saving you loads of time, and making your business work faster and smarter, too.

Having a Presentable Website

One of the most crucial dropshipping tips is to ensure your website is customer friendly. It shouldn't "scare off" a customer. Make sure your pictures, imagery, and text look professional, balanced, and that everything is triple-checked before going live. It looks unprofessional if it's not completed properly. Gaining trust is the major key.

Take a look around at other websites in your main niche. What do their websites look like? What is the product page capturing? Do their images include logos? What types of pages do they utilize? What other features or apps do they include?

A great idea is to browse through the Shopify app store to find apps that allow you to style your own store after other successful brands. You could include Instagram galleries, countdown timers, or even affiliate programs. You can also add in refund policy pages, FAQs, shipping details, and more.

Offer Awesome Customer Service

This is where many new entrepreneurs sometimes let their business down. Just because your customer has paid you the money, and you've placed the order with the supplier, this doesn't mean that you are out of the loop, altogether. Actually, if there are issues with the order, you are the one that will be held responsible in the opinion of your customer.

Be extremely proactive in your customer relations. Always follow up with customers to let them know an item has been shipped. Always offer them personal contact if they need to discuss any questions, queries, or concerns. This breeds great business for the long-term.

If possible, especially with faults, it's good to let the manufacturer handle the issue, and make sure they have your personal contact information to give to the customer, or let the manufacturer contact the client directly.

Customer service is THE secret weapon when managing a dropshipping business. It's definitely rare to get top-notch customer service from any business, these days. Spend time with your customers, and listen intently if they want to tell you something. They are, after all, the people who will buy your products. So, they matter; a lot.

- Respond fast and solve every problem with professionalism
- Surprise your customers with small gifts for staying loyal
- Don't make a customer send back a faulty product; give them a free replacement

At the end of the day, your customers are people. It is my belief that you should always treat them like you would want to be treated.

One of the best ways to stand out when selling the same products as everyone else is to offer: not great; but awesome customer service.

Helpful Tips:

1. Offering refunds for faulty products, and sending a replacement that is sound.
2. Quickly responding to customer inquiries is important. Be polite, professional, and friendly (even if they are rude or condescending).
3. Write them thank you cards if they order from your store multiple times.
4. Do monthly giveaways, only exclusive to customers who've ordered from you in the past.
5. Ensure each customer feels valued and appreciated, no matter how they behave.

Customers may not always remember what they bought from you, but they'll always remember how you treated them, that's for sure.

17

ADDITIONAL DROPSHIPPING TIPS

ONCE YOU GET GOING, DROPSHIPPING CAN BE EXTREMELY rewarding. Sometimes, you might be required to pivot as you grow your store and niche/s.

For example:

1. Your supplier might change their entire inventory, forcing you to find another supplier who does the products you are selecting.
2. A new fad might crop up within your niche that you need to add to your store immediately, so that you can capitalize on sales.
3. A product you think is awesome might not be liked by your customers, needing its removal from your store.
4. An ad you place on social media might perform spectacularly-well and require you to scale up, resulting in you negotiating for a business loan to cope with the demand.

A "pivot" isn't always good or bad, but it's a definite incorporation if you want your business to last, over time. Staying negotiable and open to change makes for great business success, long-term.

Choose ePacket

I believe ePacket shipping is the fastest and most-affordable shipping method around. And, you'll be able to ensure super-quick delivery to customers, without paying through the nose. Actually, ePacket shipping costs under $5 for most products, which is really amazing. From my own personal experience, I've seen ePacket deliveries reaching customers within 7 days, making it the best delivery method for dropshippers, overall, in my opinion.

Do Actions Daily

Any business requires daily effort. You don't need to spend 12 hours a day working on your business, but you will need to spend at least an hour or two a day on your store as you grow your sales. Each day, you'll be processing orders so that products get to your customers promptly. Make sure you always respond to customer inquiries within 24 hours (or quicker) so that customers can depend on you.

Marketing management will also need to be added in, each day. You can automate any social media postings at the beginning of the week. But, I recommend you to be active on social media, every day, so you get followers. You'll also want to be absolutely sure that your ads are always running. The more people that see you; the more conversion is possible.

Monitor the Competition

"Like" your competitors on social media. Monitor their social media and website pages regularly. Additionally, by "liking" their pages, you'll start getting their products and ads, too. What products do they advertise? Does the product get a lot of attention, such as comments or shares?

By monitoring your competition daily, you'll know which products you "should" also be selling in your store. Stay ahead of the game by knowing everything. I completely agree that, "knowledge is power." You don't want to copy your competitors, but you do want to outdo whatever they are doing, so the cash flow moves to you.

18

STEP BY STEP REITERATION

1. Choose a Product to Sell

Do this first, after researching the market. You must decide what products to sell. You also can go to trade fairs, or visit Chinese malls to get ideas about products you might want to sell. For now, let's say that you decide to sell mini espresso machines on the local marketplace.

2. Locate a Supplier who is Right for You

Find a supplier through your network, by searching on Baidu, Sohu, Google, trade fairs, etc., in your neck of the woods. Then, find a company who is interested in dropshipping these machines for you.

The company offers you a 20% commission over cost, as an example, which means that they will supply 1 mini espresso machine to you for $500.00 in USD for each item, and you should be able to retail them for 600.00 USD.

You'll need to make sure that the dropshipper has sufficient stock of the mini espresso machines on hand, so you don't end up selling a product that must be back-ordered. Then you'll also know you can keep your promises to your customers.

3. Set up an Account with the Supplier

You contact the company that can supply the espresso machines and set up a reseller account. After negotiation, you sign an agreement with them. This can be done via first visit, online, or by phone, but most companies require you to complete and return a reseller application to open an account. They might also require a tax ID, business license, or invoice.

Make sure that you agree about the period of time that you will receive the commission for. You want to feel stable in their agreed price given and your commission for each product sold by you.

4. Advertise the Product on Online Markets

Now it's time to sell the product! You advertise the product online and lure in your customers, for example; through your website, Shopify store, Amazon, or eBay, including social media advertising. The great thing is, you know what you must pay the dropshipper for the product, and you know what the minimum amount will be for the product, too.

In this case, you may start your auction at $600.00 USD since that is your cost + the margin. If you are confident that you can get more than $600.00 USD for the product you can start with a higher price, but remember, that if the product sells for less than what it costs you to fill the order, you will be losing money. Don't forget, the dropshipper will charge a shipping fee, so make sure you incorporate that into your sale.

5. When the Product Sells

I highly recommend you use instant payment methods, such as Alipay or PayPal. This allows the customer to pay you faster, which enables you to place the order with the dropshipper more quickly, which then gets the product to your customer faster.

The Order with The Dropshipper

After the customer has paid you, you must contact the dropshipper/supplier immediately to order the product on your customer's behalf. Then the dropshipper will ship the order to your customer, but under your name. Double-check their address, so no mistake on your end can occur.

An Awesome Supplier to Work with

The best supplier to partner up with:

- Must be reliable and produce quality products
- They don't have a lot of business online (filtering out competition)
- Are open for innovative ways to do business with you
- They want to outsource all online marketing tasks to you
- Are ready for growth for their company
- Can ship goods worldwide, allowing you a much bigger market
- Can ship your product/s frequently, at least once a week
- Have a physical showroom to show off their products
- Can give customer support for you, especially when you need to answer questions from customers
- Can pay your commission out on a frequent basis, without excuses

Other great tips:

1. Don't compete with your competition just on price.
2. Stick to niche products to give you the competitive edge.
3. Give superior customer service; professional, reliable and fast.
4. Sell seasonal products that big competitors might run out of.

Add Loads of Value to Stand Out from the Crowd

Dropshipping is a very competitive industry, and this is true, regardless of the niche/s you choose to sell your products in. If you focus on adding loads of value, more than anyone else in your niche area, then you'll do really well.

Adding value could include (negotiate with supplier here):

- Adding in a small free gift with your orders
- Adding handwritten notes of thanks
- Adding information guides with the purchase of a complex or technical product
- Connecting (after the sale) with customers to make sure they received their product/s and that they are happy with their purchase of your product/s

Long-Term Thinking is Crucial

If you really want to build a dropshipping business, you need to be in it for the long-haul. You should never take the "easy road" in terms of these things:

1. Don't lack in the area of product quality.

2. Only work with great, reputable suppliers.
3. Build extremely strong relationships with customers and suppliers, at all costs.

IN CONCLUSION

I would like to congratulate you for taking the time to get yourself acquainted with this massive topic of dropshipping. It's really wonderful that you are thinking of a way to make and build your wealth for your future. Once you find a great niche, a great array of suppliers, and get yourself legally viable, the world truly is your oyster.

Dropshipping is not the absolute, "get-rich-by-doing-nothing" model it has been advertised to be. In fact, if you play your cards right, it can be "the best thing since sliced bread." And I'm talking from over a decade of experience when I say this.

At the end of the day, your real success depends on how well you understand e-commerce in general. If you stick to doing the steps outlined here, and change your focus with the market, then you can have a remarkable business; one focused on growth, customer satisfaction, and great products.

As always, I am sending you every ounce of luck and my biggest, heartfelt wishes in your success as an entrepreneur. I know you can achieve anything you set out to do. The fact that you are here, speaks volumes.

Thank you, warm regards and best wishes, always, *James*.

P.S. You've got this, and you are only limited by your imagination...

P.S.S don't forget my drop-shipping list below!

I've compiled over 30 of my personal dropshipping suppliers that I've used before, based on their quality and ability. Taking the guess work out of who to choose!

Made in the USA
Middletown, DE
31 May 2018